Credit is like Pizza

A starter's guide for obtaining and maintaining credit

By T. A. Jensen

ISBN: 978-1-5307-7065-6

Table of Contents

Do you even need credit?

You are young. You don't have credit yet. You may not even know about credit. What it is or that it even exists. You have just gotten out of or are still going to high school? Maybe you have finished school and have gone to work. You want to get a place to rent? You want to buy a car? You want to rent a hotel room?

So do you know anything about credit? Heck no. You are still learning about life.

Well guess what! If you don't take the time to learn and you don't have someone to teach you about credit and finances then you are likely to make a mistake, or two, or three or a hundred.

Maybe you aren't just out of school. Maybe you just don't understand credit. No one has ever taken the time to explain but you have heard some really crazy things:

-Pay cash for everything

-Get as many credit cards as you can and always carry a balance on them

-Pay off the credit cards you have and close them as soon as they are paid.

All three of the items above are bad ideas if you wish to have a great credit score...

This silly little book will hopefully help to explain in layman's terms how, why, what, when and where's of credit.

There have been so many times that clients have sat down in front of me with credit issues, credit messes, and really big piles of debt and have then said:

"Nobody taught me"

"I turned 18 and did some really dumb things"

"My boyfriend (or girlfriend) and I took out this car loan together and then we broke up"

"I was really young and stupid and thought it wouldn't matter if I paid the bills or not"

"I don't know how any of this works"

"I got divorced and this is my ex-husband (wife's) debt and the judge said he (she) had to pay this bill"

The statements go on and on and I hear them over and over. Broken records....

It makes me nuts, crazy, loco!

Thus this little book idea seemed like a way to possibly help folks to learn a bit about this world of credit that is so complicated and complex that it takes computers to figure things out.

Basic Example: Why Credit is so important

Start with something basic:
Want to eventually buy yourself a car? If your credit sucks then your payment could be hundreds higher than if you have good credit. Doesn't matter to you? Well it might matter if you want the newest convertible but can only qualify for a tailgate on a old truck. Not the entire truck, just the tailgate!

Credit matters!

No matter what!

You think you are young and this doesn't matter because you aren't planning on doing anything for a long time. Think again! CREDIT MISTAKES take 7-10 years to go away! Think about that. If you are 18 you could potentially screw your credit up until you are 28. It really limits your options...maybe the places you can live. If you want to rent a house from a property manager, a landlord or whoever is in charge of the renting process (think apartment buildings housing complexes) then your credit will be checked out. If the only credit you have sucks then no housing for you. You might think that sleeping on your best friend's couch is a great idea now (lots of fun right?) but it likely won't be all that glamorous after a month or so. Your credit can and will likely determine if you can rent a place in your name or not. Maybe you don't care if it is rented in your name. You can just have your roommate rent it in his or her name. That is all fine and dandy as long as you have a responsible roommate who pays his or her share of the bills. Not to put a damper on roommates but I had a bunch of them and most tended to end up being a pain in the rear to live with. Maybe I was the pain the rear … (haha) but I'm going to stick to the story that my roommates were the issue and not me.

We all have or had those friends whose parents had the really awful vehicle, the one that always broke down that we really didn't want to borrow to go out because we didn't know if we would get home? Perhaps that family has or had some credit issues and could not buy anything but an old crappy car. Your credit can be a driving force in your life! Get it...car...driving force of your life? (At least one of us, me, thought that statement was funny).

What about that family who pays cash for everything? They don't have poor credit or credit issues because they paid for everything as they got it. Well guess what? If you have no credit you can't purchase a home (unless you pay cash or find a program that will allow you to "build" a credit profile from utility bills). You can't reserve a hotel room without a credit card. You can't pay for something online without credit or at the very least a debit card with a credit insignia. Everyone needs credit and if you need it you may as well take care to make sure it is good credit.

What if you have credit but never check it out? A couple of years ago I had a client who came in with a $25,000 collection account that he didn't know about. There were a couple of issues with this collection account.

1- He never signed up for the account. Hello fraud police!

2- It was a collection. Which means that his credit score is messed up because of the collection. It is also likely that he will be turned down for future credit.

3.-The size of the collection. $25,000 is a lot of cash and even if he wanted to do so he could not settle this account. It was way beyond his means to do so.

In his case he went to his local mortgage banker to apply for a home loan and found out about that he had a $25,000 collection and was denied the opportunity to buy a house with a mortgage because of it. That was a huge shock to him. He had no idea that there was a large collection on his credit.

How did he get this collection? His buddy (everyone needs a buddy like this, not!) took out a loan for $25,000 in his own name jointly with my client's name and then promptly spent the money.

How can that happen? Really? Anyone can take a loan out in your name and then not pay it back? Whoa! Scary stuff.

Here is how it went down. It was an electronic application and therefore no signature was required. According to the big bank where the loan was processed and approved there was not a signature required because it was an electronic transaction. So my client's buddy (again, everyone wishes they had friends like this, not!) goes online and applies for and gets a loan jointly with my client. My client never signed for the loan, authorized the loan, or spent any of the money associated with the loan.

You have got to be kidding me! My client never got a bill for this loan. This is typical of home loans or lines of credit that are held jointly with someone who lives at a different address. Usually the primary mortgage or loan holder will be the person who gets any correspondence concerning the mortgage or loan.

Needless to say that without clearing up this collection my client cannot buy a home, will pay much higher rates for a car loan and will be charged higher interest rates for any type of credit that he actually can qualify for.

Fortunately there are laws against this type of stuff and we were able to get the collection company to go away and stop harassing this poor man who had the buddy who messed up his "good " friend's credit.

Unfortunately most consumers (this is you or some of your friends that I'm talking about) don't know the laws, their rights or how to correct errors when it comes to their credit or their finances.

If you learn how to acquire and take care of your credit then you can use it to it's full potential! You could purchase a home, a car, go on a vacation, open a business of your own. The list goes on and on.

Let's say you NEVER want to buy anything and just want to have a place to live. IF YOUR CREDIT SUCKS YOU WILL NOT BE APPROVED BY A PROPERTY MANAGER TO RENT AN APARTMENT, HOUSE OR EVEN THE BACK OF A PICKUP TRUCK. Wait…we already stated that. It can't be said enough. CREDIT MATTERS! Yes yelling at you here.

Where do we start?

So where do we start?

When you are 18 you can legally apply for and potentially qualify for a credit card.

However there are some rules that will govern whether you may or may not have a credit card.

A few years ago any young adult who went off to attend college signed up for and got credit cards pretty much whenever this young adult wanted one.

In fact credit card companies hung out by the front doors of colleges in order to sign up young college folks fresh out of high school. I know this first hand because they were hanging out in front of the doors to my college offering many cool "gifts" for any who might choose to apply for a credit card.

Why? Do you ask, would a young college person sign up without knowing how this process works?

Free swag! Free stuff! Free coffee mugs! Free T-shirts! Free blankets with your favorite team's logo! Free autographed guitars from Eric Clapton! That last one wasn't really offered but I'm just checking to make sure you are paying attention and if you aren't sure who Eric Clapton is then Google him! He's a guitar legend (slow hand). Wow, got off topic there…oops.

I once opened a credit card account just to get the free blanket (which was given to me at the time of application by the way) of my favorite baseball team while I was at their stadium watching a game.

I still have the blanket (seven years later) and the credit card and excellent credit and other free swag (aka cool stuff) and that is totally fine if you know how to MANAGE THE FREAKING CREDIT that comes along with the cool free stuff. Am I making that sound attractive?

What was really happening when credit card companies hung out and gave college students credit cards? Most college students had no idea how to manage credit is what happened.

They took the cards, charged them up to their maximum and then stopped bothering with them.

There were and still are MILLIONS of college students who got credit cards while in college and partied, had a great time and never paid the bill. What do the students have to show for it?

Some free stuff (if their roommate didn't steal it or sell it), some got hangovers, some got dinners and some got REALLY bad CREDIT.

Disclaimer: not all roommates are bad people who steal things. No lawsuits from roommates please.

Please don't think I am bagging on every college student out there. There are of course many folks who were taught how to manage a credit card and made the payments on time and managed it all very well and have good credit.

However those students were and are the exception not the rule. I really can't count how many folks have come in to see me with a credit report that has numerous charged off credit cards who then tell me that this all happened when they were "young and stupid". Their words not mine.

So what happened to change the fallout from the college age person's '"credit card disasters"? These are my words not theirs.

A new law was created in May of 2009. It is called the CARD Act.

Card stands for Credit Card Accountability, Responsibility, and Disclosures Act.

Most of the provisions of the CARD act took effect on February 22, 2010.

Why do you, the teenager, young person, or credit newbie in this story, care at all about this CARD Act?

Well because of the free swag (aka cool stuff) that I talked about earlier....

It's not as easy now (because of the CARD Act) to get the free blanket, coffee cup, collapsible cooler, bobble head doll, voodoo pincushion, two-headed monkey or whatever else they offer up!

Since the CARD act came into law parents have to co sign on a college student's credit card if he/she is under the age of 21! "Hold on" you say? I can go to war and vote but I can't get a credit card without my parent's permission? Well it was done as a protection in hopes that a parent will monitor and not let their young adult children's credit end up all messed up as easily. It was considered by lawmakers that the credit card companies were making seriously big bucks on these cards from young folks who weren't the best managers of credit. It was also done so that the credit card companies couldn't give credit away quite as easily to young folks without credit and it also means that the parent who co-signs (in addition to the college student), is equally responsible for the credit debt incurred.

It was happening WAY too often that young people had really messed up credit by the time they were 22. Do you remember that I said earlier that it takes 7-10 years for that negative stuff (very professional term "negative stuff") to come off of your credit?

I should take a moment to point out that most things are supposed to come off of the credit bureaus in 7 years with the exception of bankruptcies. There will be more on bankruptcies at a later point.

I've been picking on college students but it isn't only college students who have been getting into trouble so young. It was anyone who was young who applied for and spent available credit to the max and didn't pay it back. It's just that at colleges and universities the students were basically preyed upon by credit card companies offering up irresistible stuff like all of the free voodoo dolls and three headed monkey prizes. What 20 year old can resist a free cup or three-headed monkey prize or for that matter anything with their school logo emblazoned on it?

Disclaimer: No lawsuits by credit card companies because I used the word "prey"

Is this law working? It may be too soon to tell...but it should help in the long run.

Until there is more education for young people with regard to managing credit and finances though, the problems will continue on.

I once did some lectures for a series of high school students on what made up their credit and how to keep the best credit score. Out of 4 classes, usually 1 class fell asleep but the other three were very engaged, and interested and were learning. At least I think they were listening. The goal of having these discussions and presentations was to hopefully help one student, or many students, keep away from the pitfalls of not understanding credit and how to manage it.

I personally think the CARD act is good in most ways but it is still relatively new. Time will tell I suppose. Again this is my personal opinion. No opinion bashing please.

FICO Score

Okay so what makes up a credit score and why does that matter?

FICO is the premiere credit scoring company used in the USA for lending decisions. FICO is a mathematical algorithm. It takes everything on a credit report and throws it together and spits out a number.

There are many other scoring "models" and systems out there in the marketplace but FICO is generally used by most lending institutions in the USA.

With FICO the higher the number the better the score. FICO scores can range from 300 to 850.

In all of my years of banking and lending I have never seen a lower score than 400 or a higher score than 835. Mathematically it just isn't probable, but they could be out there somewhere. " Over the rainbow" perhaps?

There are so many working parts to the mathematical algorithms in the FICO scoring machines that is would be highly unlikely to achieve an 850 score.

Your FICO credit score is made of 5 components, and within those five components there are a LOT of sub components....

Remember that most consumer lenders of money in the USA use this model of (FICO) scoring to determine their lending decisions.

The FICO (which is a registered trademark by the way) score is the most widely used credit-scoring model in the

USA. Most lenders use FICO. FICO is a company that had used algorithms to determine and compile credit scores for many years. Their methods whether you like them or not are a lending industry standard and they have set the bar for all credit scoring models. There are many versions of FICO software.

FICO 08

FICO for auto dealers

FICO for mortgage lenders

There are many versions of FICO and they are industry specific. We will discuss this in more detail later.

So let's say you need to finance the newest fastest crotch rocket motorcycle or the newest laptop, IPAD, IPOD, cell phone, pair of pants or whatever...

With a 740 FICO score you likely can get the best interest rate...let's say it's a 1.5% special offer (auto loan as an example.

Now let's say that you have a 600 FICO score. You may not get the money to borrow at all or you may be offered it at a rate of say 18% or 28%.

"So what?" you say. Let me tell you what! Listen up! MONEY????????? You won't be able to afford the crotch rocket at 18% or 28% and will have to settle for maybe a scooter or your friend's broken down laptop or thrift store pants or whatever. Not that there is anything wrong with thrift store pants or any of the above items... some of my best friends have thrift store pants that are very nice.

Let's go back to the laptop as an example:

If said laptop cost $2,000 and you have one year to pay for it the payments would be as follows:

$2,000	1.5%	payment $168.02
$2,000	18%	payment $183.36
$2,000	28%	payment $193.01

Let's give this to you in hard numbers.

$2,000 at 1.5% in one year with payments of $168.02 means that the laptop cost only $2,016.24. That totals only $16.24 more than the actual sticker price.

Now let's look at the same $2,000 over the same year at 28%. $2,316.12. Over $316.12 more for the laptop than the actual sticker price. We are talking about a really tricked out lap top by the way...very tricked out for $2,000 I'm thinking.

Doesn't seem like that much difference in payment? Let's compare a loan of $15,000 (the new motorcycle or car that you would like) on a 3 year (or 36 month) payment term

$15,000	5%	payment $449.56
$15,000	18%	payment $542.29
$15,000	28%	payment $620.45

Hard numbers time again.

$15,000 at 5% over 36 months: Total payments at $449.56 come to $16,184.28.

Not bad. Only costing $1,618.43 to use someone else's $15,000 for 3 years.

Now the 28% scenario:

$15,000 at 28% (and I know clients of mine who have auto loans at 28% because of their credit scores) payment is $620.45 comes to a total of $22,336.34

Hmmm...let's see. A total of $1,618.43 to use someone

14

else's $15,000 or a total of $7,336.34 to use someone else's $15,000. Quite a difference!

Not to mention that the monthly payment is almost $170 per month more at the higher interest rate.

Makes a pretty big difference in the payment amount doesn't it?

The credit issues that befall most people's credit are usually preventable and strategically you can have good credit. I'm going to give you the strategy and help to prevent a bad credit score.

How does FICO figure it out?

FICO writes software to determine what things folks have in common...

It's the "predictability" that a consumer will become 90 days or more delinquent on an obligation.

Every so often FICO grabs a few million credit reports and compares the things that folks with delinquencies (late payments, judgments, collections, repossessions, etc) in common.

Are most folks with a 30 day late payment maxed out on their credit cards? It's these similarities that help to determine how much weight to give the factors that are part of a credit score.

It's all mathematics!!! Don't like math? You don't have to! FICO does it for ya...

It's a lot like Pizza

Let's think of a FICO score as a big pizza pie. The pizza pie is divided into five segments.

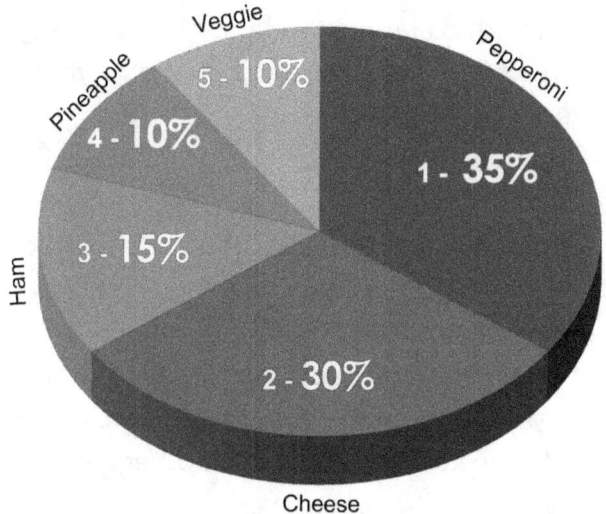

In this FICO pizza person world there are five different people vying for a slice of that pizza.

The person who gets the biggest piece of the pizza is the one that matters the most in this FICO person pizza world.

Let's say that largest piece is pepperoni—35% of the pizza- Pepperoni is also known as the segment that refers to Past delinquencies. —Payment history.

What does the history of the accounts in your credit profile show? Have they been paid on time? Are there any collections? Any judgments? Any Charge-offs? Any tax liens?

Any credit card accounts? Mortgage accounts? Auto loans? —If there are, have they been paid on time? Have they been late?

Let's say the second largest is Cheese—30% of the pizza—Cheese is also known as the segment that refers to revolving debt ratio.

In a nutshell it is how much revolving credit do you have available for use?

Let's say the third largest is Ham—15% of the pizza— Ham is also known as the segment that refers to the average age of a credit file.

How long has your credit been established? Is the existing credit new?

Let's say that one of the small pieces is Pineapple—10% of the pizza—Pineapple is also known as the segment that refers to the mix or type of credit.

Is all of your credit profile made up of credit cards?

Now we should name the last piece of the pizza. Let's see…we really need to make it special. Veggie. Veggie is the red piece of our little pizza party.

Everyone loves their veggies, right? It's that small slice next to the Pepperoni slice.

It is also 10% of the pizza. It refers to the number of inquiries on your credit profile. It is one of the most misunderstood segments in the credit profile and it will be discussed at length further.

Pepperoni Pizza

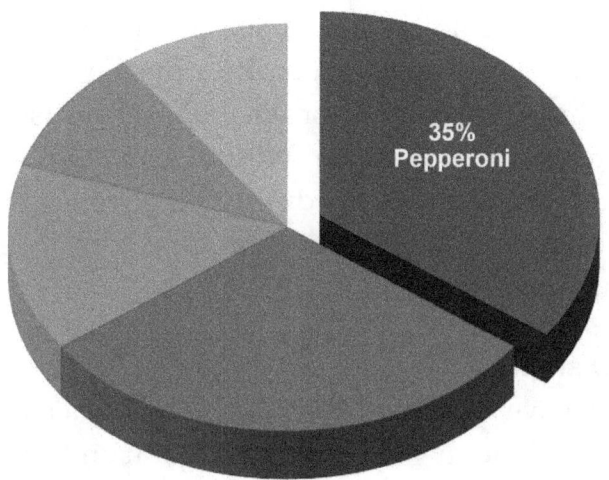

Figure 1
35% Payment History—Pepperoni part of pizza

Pepperoni—also known as the Past Delinquencies section of the FICO pizza pie…approximately 35% of the FICO credit scoring model.

35% of your FICO score is made up of past delinquencies.

Past delinquencies include:

-payment history

-date of last activity or payment

-level of delinquency (30 days behind , 60 days behind etc)

-timing of delinquency

-type of payment missed

What the heck does all of that mean?

First: payment history—have you made your payments on time? Specifically have the payments been made on or before the due date or less than 30 days past the due date. A mortgage payment has a due date and is generally considered late 15 days after the due date (which will result in a late payment penalty). In the "Pepperoni" world though it is only considered late if it is 30 days or more past the due date. With that in mind, NEVER make the payment past the due date if possible. Why pay late fees and or extra interest on something unless it is absolutely necessary.

Real example:

Ok! You have a buddy named John who has a credit card from bank X. John your buddy just got it and hasn't had credit before.

John is taking all of his pals out for dinner and buying everyone new jackets... It's odd to buy Jackets for your friends but that is what John does!

John never plans on paying back the institution who gave him the credit card. He has never been taught about this. No big deal right?

So John and his buddies (which includes you. Yahoo!) go out and have a fabulous time with no thought whatsoever to payment for the goods. In this case the goods are dinner and a coat. It's a good deal for you. Not so much for John. It's not your problem! It's your new best buddy John's card after all. What do you care?

Well it really isn't your responsibility but morally you should care but that is another discussion we have to have later in another book.

So back to best buddy John. He gets the bill for the credit card and decides, "screw you bank, institution or whoever you are" "I'm not paying for this". At this point a few things happen.

30 days after the payment due date if no payment has been made then the card has a "30 day" delinquency. It is now showing on your credit profile as a delinquent payment or a late payment. Pepperoni piece of pizza is now a little unhappy.

Along with this delinquency there will be lovely phone calls coming into John's phone number that he put on the application. The phone calls will be numerous, annoying and coming at all hours.

Next step:
Still no payment is made and another 30 days goes by. Now it is a "60 day" delinquency or a "60 day late". Pepperoni is even more unhappy which isn't a good thing in FICO pizza person world.

More phone calls come to John from the institution/ bank.

Another 30 days go by, and now it's a 90 day delinquency. By this time best buddy John is getting millions of phone calls asking him to pay up. Ok so maybe a million is a bit of an exaggeration but it might seem like a million calls! The calls are annoying him but he soon learns to recognize the number and not answer the calls.

Another 30 days goes by and good old Johnnie hasn't made a single payment to the institution/bank and he really doesn't answer any of the annoying phone calls. This is officially 180 days behind in making payments and at that time usually a bank/credit card issuer will begin the process of sending the card to a collection agency or selling the debt to a collection agency and "charging off" or putting "profit and loss" status on the debt.

Pepperoni FICO pizza person is really not all that impressed which is really now putting a lot of stress on that 35% piece of the pizza.

So let's get back to the credit report, the credit score and what this whole scenario has done or potentially done to best buddy (now known as not very smart with his credit John) John's credit.

The most important part of your Pepperoni credit score is payment history (approximately 35%) and not very smart John has just messed his only payment history up. He has late payments, then a debt that has been charged off or sent to collection (more about collections later).

35% of his score is now RADICALLY MESSED UP.

It will likely remain on his credit report for 7 years and also have a negative impact his credit score for that length of time (the amount that it impacts his score will lessen over time but it will have some type of impact for as long as it remains on the credit report/profile.

Within the 35% Pepperoni section (Past delinquencies) there are a number of other factors considered (as mentioned above).

The timing of the delinquency—the more recent the negative payment history the more it impacts the credit score. In other words it will slowly fade into the sunset over the seven years but as said before it will still have some impact.

A year goes by since John has not made any attempt to pay off this credit card so it impacts Pepperoni pizza slice a little less. It is still messing up the Pepperoni just not quite as much as it did right after it happened. Unless John does this again with another debt and then it becomes an even bigger issue. See below.

The number of accounts with delinquencies has an impact as well. If there are numerous accounts with past delinquencies it will have potentially a larger impact on your credit score. Have one account as a collection or charge off or judgment and you have one problem with Pepperoni slice. Have three and Pepperoni has three problems which will multiply depending on the rest of the credit profile.

The level of delinquency is another factor in the Pepperoni world—not so smart with his credit John missed his first payment. A 30 day delinquency.

A 30 day is the lowest level of delinquency on the meter. The further behind you get, the faster you go down the tubes. Ok not very well articulated (bad grammar). Let's try this:

The longer the payment goes unpaid the larger impact it has on the credit score. The higher the delinquency level the more it impacts your credit score in a negative way.

If it goes to collection it is yet another level (and not a good one) of delinquency. If it is charged off by—the bank or credit card issuer or whoever issued to credit, then it again is a different level of delinquency.

By the way a charge-off is a debt that is considered "uncollectible" by the creditor who owns the debt.

YAHOO!!! Uncollectible! Mr. Smarty pants John is off the hook. NOT LIKELY sport.

It can still be collected, sold to another collection agency and go on and on and on.

Oh and did I mention it stays on your credit for 7+ years?

The last activity date—another piece of Pepperoni FICO pizza person—the last payment made on the account is usually the last activity

Did I mention that if smarty pants John still doesn't pay the bill that he could get taken to court? Any owner of the debt could go to court and get a judgment against him. The judgment could result in wages being garnished! Oh, and did we mention that a judgment is usually put on your credit as well and is another form of delinquency?

The type of payment you miss also has an impact on the credit score. For example a mortgage payment (the loan that allows you to borrow to purchase a house) is more important to Mr. FICO pepperoni person than a credit card payment.

Why is that? Well a mortgage is a much larger obligation usually and is weighted more heavily.

So how do you make Pepperoni FICO pizza person happy? 35% is the most greedy part of the credit score... It's easy really.

Pay your bills on time. It is as simple as that.

Pay any bill you get before the due date preferably. Never miss a payment. If you have to miss a payment call the creditor first and see if you can set something up in advance with them so that they know you are missing the payment.

I keep talking about banks/credit card companies but there are many other things that can show up on your credit if you don't pay them. We will save that for another chapter.

8

Cheese Pizza

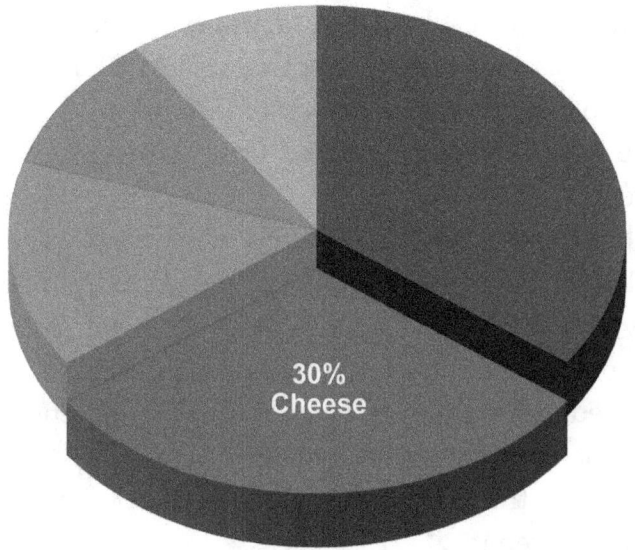

Figure 2 30% Debt Ratio—Cheese portion of pizza

Cheese please—second largest piece.

30% of the credit score is Cheese pizza person—the one everyone loves unless they don't. Who doesn't like cheese anyway? I mean I am literally part rat because I love cheese so much. I personally know two little boys who don't like cheese and I just don't understand them. Wow.

Oops, I got distracted by the cheese. I'm sure that I could just eat cheese and remain alive forever…

The second piece of the pie on your credit reports are called debt ratio.

The debt ratio or the cheese in this diagram makes up 30% of your credit score.

So what the heck is a debt ratio and why does that matter in your credit score?

Well let's see is we can make it simple.

Note to those who have every applied for a mortgage and have heard that their "debt-ratio is 35%". In this case debt ratio has nothing to do with mortgages.

You got that wonderful credit card when you went to college

A limit was issued on that wonderful card. The limit was $1,000. A one thousand dollar line of credit to do with what you want and to have fun with! Whatever you want! As long as it's legal that is! May I hear a YAHOO!!

Immediately you and your buddies/girlfriends went out and had an absolute blast and charged it up to $1,000.

Hmmm…this time maybe you all went to the concert at the local arena.

Tickets: $300, shirts $300, food $300 (easy to do in an arena) and $100 in snacks.

When the bill comes did you have the $1,000 to pay it off? Probably not! If you have that kind of money just lying around you wouldn't need the credit card would you?

Anyway, if the card is charged up to it's full limit it is 100% maxed out. The "debt ratio" for the credit scoring system reads it as 100%. One thousand available and one thousand used or owed.

Let's go back to math class for a moment. Sorry about that. Please don't go running and screaming from the room. It won't hurt that much, if at all, to do this math.

The same card for an example:

You and your same friends only charge $100 on that same card. You decide that instead of going to the concert you go have hot wings at the local eatery/bar. Only if you are old enough can you go to the local pub but let's pretend that you are old enough and the local pub (you are 21 in this scenario and therefore allowed into a pub) has amazing hot wings and great TVs and great service and that you are all so happy to go for wings that it does the trick! Whew tiring.

    Note: no suing the author over a suggestion that a "young" adult would go to a bar. It's just an example folks. If you don't like pubs or bars then just think of a nice little restaurant in it's place. **

    ANYWAY....back to the scenario

    We divide that $100 hot wing bill into the $1,000 limit on that card ($900 of the card limit is still available because you only spent $100) and voila (again that math thing) you have a 10% debt ratio on your credit score.

    Told you the math would be easy.

    The lower the debt ratio on your credit the better your credit score will be. In other words the less that you have owing versus what you have available on the card or line of credit the better your FICO cheese pizza will taste. The FICO cheese pizza person likes it when you don't owe much on revolving credit. Revolving simply means that you can use the line of credit over and over (like a credit card).

    NOTE: Most revolving debt is in the form of credit card debt but occasionally a line of credit is issued and a line of credit would count in this equation as well (as long as it isn't listed as a mortgage).

Well why the heck does the credit scoring system, aka FICO cheese pizza person give a hoot about how much or your revolving credit is used versus what is available? Why does FICO pizza cheese person only want you to go out for hot wings and not to the concert?

Because statistically, again that math thing, if you have a high debt ratio (revolving credit usage) then you are more likely to default on your payments. It is flat out just more statistically probable.

Over the years FICO has compiled statistics. Many statistics. One of the statistics that rings true over and over is that if your credit cards (revolving credit) is maxed out (you are using all of what is available) then you highly likely to default on your payments.

It has been and likely always will be a huge part of your credit score.

What can you do to make sure that you get the most out of this part of your credit score? Pay your credit cards off when you get the bill. This will ensure a healthy debt ratio on your credit score. It will also ensure that you don't pay the bank any interest charges or fees that as a result creates extra income for the bank. Banks and lenders love customers who do not pay off their revolving credit every month.

Interest accumulates quickly and at times interest rates can be raised resulting in even more interest that the institution just pockets. Millions and millions in bank revenue comes from the interest paid on revolving credit every year.

If you are late on a revolving credit payment then not only is interest charged but you will also be charged a late fee. Then interest will accumulate on the late fee as well as the balance as well as any unpaid interest. Major snowball of fees here folks.

It's like being charged for the bun when you buy a hotdog. Why do you want to pay for a bun when the hotdog is supposed to come with one? Same with unnecessary bank fees. Don't pay them anything extra if at all possible…not necessary.

This is one of the very largest misconceptions in the credit card/revolving credit world. Advice is given out by lenders and many others that it is better for your credit score to carry a balance on credit cards. "Leave at least 20% owing on your credit cards. It will help your score". This is NOT true. Did you read that? NOT TRUE. I have discussed this numerous times with a friend of mine who is a nationally renowned credit expert. In fact he used to work for one of the credit bureaus. He has said that it "might" be slightly better to carry 1% of the available credit as a balance but the results are very negligible (if all other things are considered equal). If you do carry a balance though you will be pay interest. ***See previous paragraph about hotdog and bun***

FICO released a study in 2012 that found the people with the very highest scores have an average revolving debt ratio of no more than 7%. Seven percent!!! That's a little tiny sliver of cheese pizza.

Math again: that means with a card of $100 they carry no more than a $7 balance. Most people with the highest scores in the nation have the rest of the pizza figured out as well and don't carry any balance on a bunch of credit cards or may have a tiny balance on one when the credit is pulled. We may discuss that in more detail in another section.

Since I am a former banker I am totally against paying any interest or any fees to any banking institution. Sometimes you have no way around paying interest. In most cases if you need a car or a house you will likely borrow money and pay interest in order to obtain either one. But in the case of credit cards you really shouldn't be using them unless you can pay them off. It takes some willpower sometimes.

I can't tell you how many times I have seen clients with $30,000 or $40,000 in credit card debt. They will either be paying the balances for the rest of their lives or have stopped paying them altogether and have collections and charge offs as a result.

Guess what folks…if you have collections and charge offs then pepperoni pizza guy isn't happy and your pizza is going to turn rancid very quickly. Yucky.

It would be very interesting to find out exactly what people have to show for a $40000 credit card debt. Most haven't purchased cars with their cards. Or paid medical bills.

Most have been STUFF. That is a lot of stuff…wow.

Jumping on the soap box here. Please don't charge up thousands and thousands of dollars of credit card debt. You will never remember the extra pair of shoes, bag, jeans, or whatever that you are using it for. There really isn't much good than can come of it. If you have the money to pay it off every month then knock yourself out. Otherwise please try to stay away from overuse.

Real Scenario:

Client has a credit card that has a $1000 limit and another one that has a $500 limit. Client is currently carrying balances of $875 on the first card (with the $1,000 limit) and carrying a balance of $400 on the card that has the $500 limit which means that both cards are being used quite heavily. The cards are then paid off and the client waits until it reports to the credit reporting agencies to have his credit re-pulled by the bank who he is trying to get his loan with. The cards are now showing zero balances on the new credit report. Everything else was equal. No other new credit, no late payments. Nothing but the balances of the credit cards changed. The credit score jumped by 30 points in this particular case. ** Remember the higher the credit score the better rates you should get when borrowing**

Each case is different and each credit score is different but it can make a very large difference, sometimes, when credit card balances are paid off.

9

Ham pizza

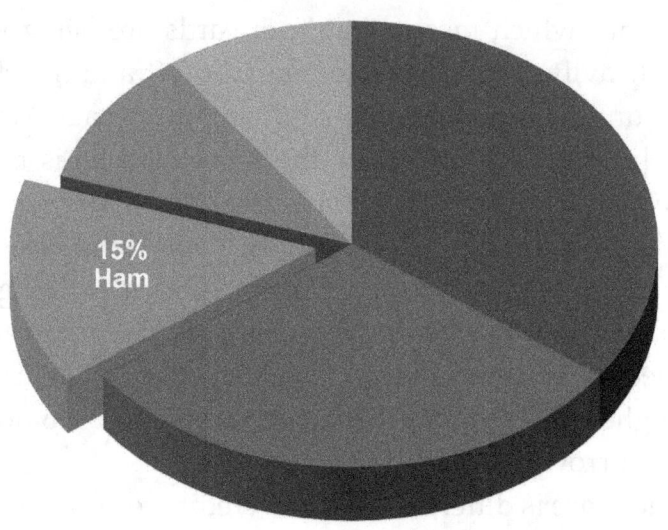

Figure 3 15% Average Age of Credit File—Ham portion of Pizza

The next part of your credit score is the average age of the credit files. It accounts for 15% of the credit score. We will call is the ham portion of the lovely pizza. In this illustration pretend the ham is green. Cue Dr. Seuss!

Oh wait! That's green eggs and ham. Is the ham green in Green Eggs and Ham?

Wow! I got way off topic here.

Let's get back to the boring but important stuff. How does the ham (the Average age of credit file) impact the pizza (credit score)?

This part of the score means that the longer you have had credit the better your credit score will be. That may be hard to do just coming out of high school or when you first become employed because your credit will be new credit. Or you won't have any that has an age.

Again: with the statistics stuff. In FICO's scoring models more emphasis is given to lines of credit, mortgages, or any other type of credit for that matter, the longer it has been in existence. It has been shown statistically that the longer someone has had credit the less likely they are to default on that said credit.

It's all a numbers game ladies and gentlemen. All about statistics as pointed out earlier and will be pointed out again and again in this FICO pizza person model of credit.

Remember how we talked about piggybacking off of a parent to get some credit history? This not only helps to build up credit history from a standpoint of new credit but it also helps the ham to be less rotten.

Piggybacking is best if done with a credit card that has some seasoning. Not seasoning like salt, seasoning like time. The older the card the better it will be for the ham portion of the pizza.

Once you do get your own credit card this is one reason to keep it open. To build up time and have "seasoned" credit cards or other credit. It all helps to get the highest score possible and helps the ham to not go rotten. Nice image eh?

Recap: If piggybacking off of a parent or relative, Try to piggyback with a card that is older. It helps the 15% average age of the file part of the credit score. That is the ham in the FICO pizza person's pie.

Keep credit cards even if paid off. Keep them open though (and use them once a year). It also helps with the average age of your credit profile.

15% isn't nearly as big of a piece of the pizza as the Pepperoni (payment history) or the Cheese (revolving debt ratio) but it is an important piece of the pizza just the same.

10

Pineapple Pizza

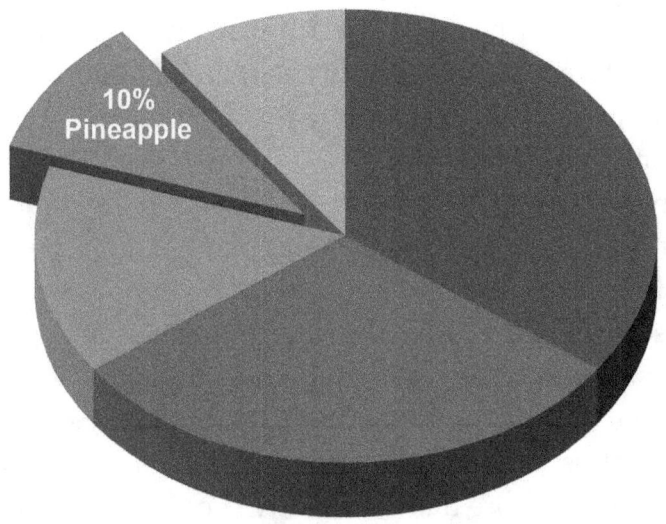

Figure 4- 10% Mix of Credit or Pineapple on the pizza

Now let's talk about the next piece of the FICO person pizza pie. Pineapple. We had ham so we had to have pineapple. It just doesn't go with just ham and no pineapple.

Also known as Mix or types of credit.

Basically again statistically if you have different types of credit it statistically has been shown that you know how to manage your credit better.

Why would you want a plain pizza when you can have ham, cheese, pepperoni and pineapple? Same goes with the Pineapple portion of the FICO pizza person pie.

A few different types of credit will help to even out the score and makes you less likely to default.

It's all about the stats (math and statistics).

It is good to have a mix of credit. A car/auto loan a mortgage loan a few credit cards.

The folks who have the highest FICO scores don't have just a couple of credit cards in their history.

But again this is something that is going to take time. It is only 10% of the score but 10% can be very important when another area of the score is lacking. It all adds up when the whole pizza it put together.

How do you get an auto loan, a mortgage and credit cards? This will again take time and take starting from the smallest item and working your way up.

It will take some credit history usually to get an auto loan (unless you get one with quite a high rate which is again paying more than you really should). Starting with the credit cards as discussed in previous chapters. Once you have obtained some credit history then you will be more likely to qualify to buy a car and obtain a car loan.

Once you have had some history with the time that you have maintained a good credit history then you may qualify for a mortgage. There are many other things that determine if you can qualify for a mortgage but having depth of credit (credit that has been around for a while and a variation of credit) are usually fairly big parts of obtaining mortgage loans.

11

Veggie Pizza

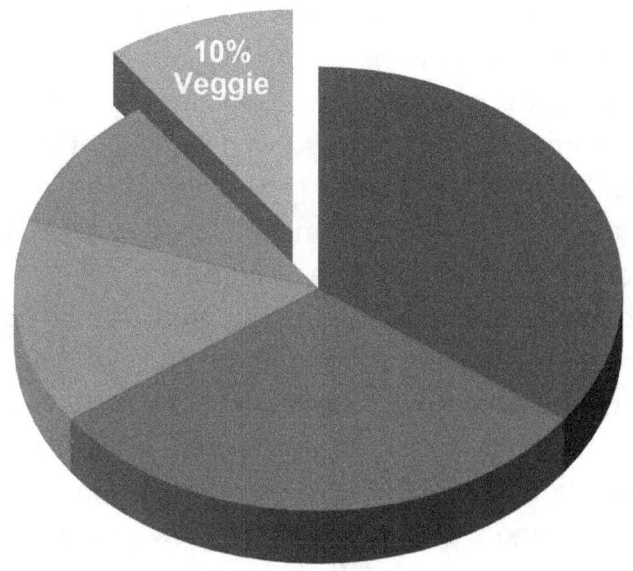

INQUIRIES: 10% of Credit Scores—Veggie Pizza

Let's call this last piece the pie veggie. Everybody loves veggie pizzas right?

The last part of the credit score is inquiries. This particular part gets a lot of press! Many people talk about it. Many people get the information WRONG!

As a newer credit holder you will have to be careful about this category.

Inquiries, refers to the terminology given to the event that occurs every time credit is applied for. Wow. That sentence confused me! How about you?

Let's try again. Every time an application for a credit card is processed the credit card company requests a credit report from the credit bureaus to see if the applicant fits into the box of credit worthiness that the particular credit card company requires.

These credit pulls/requests are called hard inquiries. They can impact your credit score negatively if the credit is pulled too often. The same types of inquiries are made if you apply for a mortgage, an auto loan, a personal loan, a line of credit and numerous other things.

Each inquiry is counted in the credit score up to a maximum of 10 inquiries. Once there are 10 inquiries the "damage" or maximum impact to FICO is done. No more will be counted against the credit score. This is all within a 12 month period however....so every month the inquiries from a year ago will fall off and any new ones will again impact the credit score.. **It is important to note that the "twelve month" period refers to the 12 months prior to and including the inquiry date. **

There are two types of credit inquiries that count as one inquiry. One is an application for a mortgage and the second is an application for an automotive loan.

You may have multiple inquiries for a mortgage or an auto loan and in any 45 day period they will only count as one inquiry.

This is because the credit score system recognizes that consumers should be able to shop for an auto loan or a mortgage loan without being penalized. The shopping is basically impact free (on the inquiry part of the FICO

Pizza veggie pie). However it is only "impact free" for 45 days. For example: If you apply today and then apply for a mortgage again 60 days later (which requires another credit inquiry) it will count as another hard inquiry. One that may impact the FICO credit score!

With inquiries there are some things that won't impact the credit score even though an inquiry has been done on your credit.

One is for a job. Many banks, school districts, police departments, cities, fire departments and many more will pull credit for anyone who applies for a job. After all you really don't the want the person at the bank handling your money to be someone who has never paid a bill on time in their life!

Another is in the case of insurance companies. All insurance companies pull credit for auto insurance for example.

Rental agencies who manage rental properties often pull credit as well to make sure that another landlord hasn't placed a claim against you or that you don't just have pages of collections on your credit (an unlikely candidate to pay rent on time do ya think?)

Also if you get a credit card application in the mail that says your are "pre-approved" the credit card company has likely pulled credit for this offer.

How can they do this without your permission?

These inquiries are called "soft inquiries". They DO NOT have an impact on your credit score. These type of inquiries are definitely helpful for the folks requesting the credit check and they don't hurt you.

In fact many of those inquiries don't even produce credit scores. The insurance companies all have their own scoring system (remember those different systems for different industries? Oh wait, I haven't explained that yet. DUH!) and that system doesn't produce a FICO score. That system produces a score that is specific to insurance companies and is mostly looking for claims, missed payments etc. If you miss your car payment for example you are more likely to be a dud when it comes to making the insurance payment...Just my opinion.

Many things can impact credit scores in minor ways. The combination of how long items have been open, or active, or last active, or last charged on or the original amount of a loan or many combinations of things.

The big 3

In some circles you might hear the term "the big three" when discussions of credit reporting agencies arises.

There are many different credit reporting agencies or credit bureaus as they are commonly called.

The largest 3 by far are Trans Union, Experian and Equifax.

These three are the primary consumers of FICO software and are the primary source for the actual credit scores that are used in the lending circles for consumer lending.

When you hear the term my Experian score is _____. That is the specific credit reporting agency or bureau that issued that particular score.

All three bureaus will have scores that are independent of each other. All three bureaus charge for the issuance of scores. What the heck kind of word is issuance anyway?

The big 3 are very wealthy and powerful and an integral part of the US lending industry.

-13-
How do I get credit when I don't have any?

Let's start at the beginning. You have just turned 18 and are legally able to borrow money and to take out credit. It is likely that you have no credit at this time. Unless of course, someone has stolen your identity but we will get to that in another chapter.

There are a few steps that you can take when you are 18 that will allow you to build credit and build a credit score.

1- Go get a secured credit card from a bank or credit union or credit card company.

Secured credit cards are an actual credit card and most banks/credit unions or credit card companies offer them.

Why would they do that when I've been telling you that you need a good credit score to obtain credit?

The secured part of the Secured Credit Card is the key.

When opening a secured credit card you need to put a deposit into an account at one of these aforementioned institutions. The funds that are deposited are held and they "secure" the credit card. You cannot close the account. You cannot withdraw from or have access to the funds in the account. You cannot do anything to the account unless the credit card is paid and closed or converted to an unsecured credit card. The money in the account secures the credit card and therefore poses the banking institution no risk. If you don't pay your credit card bill the credit card issuer simply takes the money from your account to pay off the debt.

Secured credit cards are wonderful for establishing credit. Almost everyone qualifies (unless there are a number of derogatory items showing unpaid on your credit profile) and all you need to do is to deposit money in an account to secure the credit card.

Usually after a period of time (sometimes as quickly as a year) the funds are released and the credit card can then stand on it's own without funds securing it. The policy of releasing the funds and letting the card stand on it's own vary from institution to institution so you need to check that out before assuming anything.

2- If you have a close family member who has a card with a LOW or ZERO balance and a GOOD payment history then you can be added to that account as an authorized user.

Notice I capitalize LOW or ZERO balance.

Low balance—definition—less than 10% of the available credit limit that's owing on the credit card. Note: That is only my opinion of a "low balance"

Zero balance—definition—well if I need to explain that then we need to talk some more about other things in your life.

Good payment history—no late payments at all or at the very least in the last 24 months. If the credit card has a higher balance, or a poor payment history it will actually hurt your credit.

So the conversation with close family member goes something like this.

"Mom, I read that you should put me on your paid off and open credit card that has a zero balance as an authorized user"

Mom replies " No freaking way I am giving you my

credit card or access to it"

"You are only 18 and you will charge my card to the max and then I'll owe a big bill and then I'll have to disown you and adopt the kid down the street"

Well only part of the last statement actually came from mom....

There is a wonderful answer to mom's concerns though.

First of all the word AUTHORIZED is a huge factor when adding someone to a credit card account.

An authorized user is allowed access to use of the credit account only. In other words

an authorized user is:

-not financially responsible for the account

-can be added at any time

-can be removed at any time

-usually, doesn't require an inquiry (potentially can be damaging) in order to be added to the account

The other beautiful thing about an authorized user is they cannot:

-ask for limit increases

-make any changes to the terms, or anything else on the card

-cannot add or remove another user to or from the account

-cannot close the account

I tell parents all the time to add a child as an authorized user to build credit but to NOT give them a card. The child has no need for the card. The only reason we are adding the child is to "piggyback" the credit history over from the family member.

Of course if mom, dad or family member want to give junior a card that is up to that parent but said parent should beware that if junior possesses the card then junior can use the card...say to charge the new $200 pair of jeans at the mall?

Bad credit history can be piggybacked over and damage a credit score as well. So I say again that it is really important to make sure that the card has great payment history.

If something happens and a payment is missed the authorized user can be removed from the card (again by the primary card holder) and thereby removing the poor payment history.

We once (when I was in the mortgage lending business) had to have someone removed from being an authorized user because the actual cardholder (I think it was my client's moms credit card) had not made the payments on time. It took about 45 days to remove the authorized user and then voila, the credit score went up and all was well!

Piggyback good credit card with low or no balance— GOOD

Piggyback credit card with bad payment history or high balance—BAD

3. Get a small loan against your car if you have one. Sometimes a bank will give a fairly new borrower a small loan, $1,000 or $2,000 as a signature loan. This small loan will give a nice bit of stability to a credit profile that is lacking in depth. It will be very important to pay the loan back in a timely fashion. Make the payments on time or before they are due.

4. Have a family member co-sign for a loan. Before I give this as an example to build credit I feel that it is necessary to really emphasize that I do not like co-signing. If you or your mom or anyone else ever comes

to me and asks me whether they should co-sign a loan for someone I am going to tell them NO! Why would I say this is a way to build credit when I would advise against it? WELLLLL... (imagine me drawling out that word for a while) it's because I have seen too many people get burned by co-signing for someone else.

What is co-signing? It means that someone is really applying for the loan or financing jointly (very key word) with someone else. There are a couple of issues with co-signing.

People who co-sign for someone else often think that for some reason they are just putting their lovely signature on a piece of paper. Really they are jointly (there is that word again) applying for the financing.

If said person who you are "co-signing" for doesn't make his or her payments on time then YOU as co-signer would have to make the payment or be responsible for the payment.

"But I'm only a co-signer" you scream in anguish. "I'm not responsible for their loan I didn't get the money

If payments are not made the late payment history will also be reported on your credit. You co-signed and you legally have to pay back to debt.

Other things that can and may appear on a credit profile

There are numerous things that only "sometimes" appear on a credit report. Talk about confusing! Just when I tell you how to handle things I then turn around and say that "sometimes" things just appear? It's not a magic trick. REALLY!!!

<u>Medical bills</u>

Medical bills usually only appear on a credit report if they have been turned over to a collection company. Note to self and to you dear reader: medical bills are sometimes an unavoidable part of life. If something medically happens to you or your family and as a result you incur a medical bill that you don't have the funds to pay then immediately contact the creditor who issued the bill.

#1- They may have some of your information wrong and because of that your insurance rejects the claim. Disclaimer: This is assuming you had insurance and assuming that the insurance was supposed to pay for part of it.

Note: I can get up on a big soapbox about this topic. 2nd Note: Don't know what a soapbox is? Google it!! Common saying "Get down off of your soapbox!"

This recently happened to ME!!!!! The lab that performed the blood work on my annual checkup had my birthdate wrong and because of that my medical insurance rejected the payment. Once the right birthdate was entered it was paid by my insurance.

#2- If you have some of the funds to pay the bill, sometimes a collection company will take a partial payment in lieu of the full amount.

#3- Ask the billing agency (the hospital or whoever it may be) if they will allow you to make monthly payments to them. USUALLY they won't turn it over to collection agency as long as you stick to payment arrangements and are not late in making payments on said arrangement.

#4- New guidelines are coming being adopted regarding medical collections that have been paid (by insurance). It is believed that the credit bureaus will delete these type of collections from their reports. It remains to be seen how and if the credit bureaus will be able to tell the difference between a medical bill that is paid by insurance or by a consumer.

There may be more changes that will occur with regard to medical bills and the credit reporting agencies but nothing is definite as of this printing.

Cell phone bill—only reports to a credit report if turned in to collection

Utility bills—only reports if a collection

Unpaid rent—only if in collection

Student loans—report usually and can help credit score values if paid on time. Will hurt if not paid on time or if they go into collection, cannot be discharged in a bankruptcy. You are stuck with them.

Catalog/internet companies—usually only report if it goes to collection

State, federal, city, county taxes—only reported if they go to a lien or a judgment

Parking tickets—Yup you guessed it...if you are bad and don't pay the ticket. It will likely go on your credit.

Court fines—Can be turned over to collection in some cases as well.

There are numerous other items that could be sent to a collection agency if you don't pay the bill. I can't think of them right now! LOL!

Disclaimer: If you are unaware of the VERY casual LOL meaning please Google it!

15

The CARD act

Let's go back to that CARD act we talked about earlier. There are a few other things that came out of that act other than just protecting youngsters from being bombarded at college. Here is a brief rundown.

1- Credit card companies generally cannot increase interest rates on existing balances unless the cardholder has missed 2 consecutive payments—HELLO, make your payments on time!

2-Card issuers can increase rates on new purchased providing that they give the cardholder 45 days advance warning of the rate increase.

3-Credit card bills must be due the same date each month and the consumer must have at least 21 days to pay their bill. Before this law the dates didn't often match and sometimes a bill would arrive and be due (or late) the next week.

4- Over limit fees. I love this one. These fees come because some consumers have routinely gone over the set limit on their credit cards. This was a free pass for the Credit Card issuer to tack on some fees and make a bunch of extra money.

Here is a quick example:

Let's use a credit card with a $1,000 limit. As the consumer Joe has gone to "Jamaica mon" and wants to buy himself the latest Zip line tour. His card has already got a one thousand ($1,000) owing but he doesn't know it because he is on vacation he doesn't really care. He's been having fun and that is REALLY all that matters to him.

Prior to the CARD act becoming law his card would have allowed the transaction to go through and then he would unknowingly be charged some lovely (aka HIGHJ) "over the limit" fees. Oops...but wait, Joe didn't even know he was over limit. Too bad so sad for Joe!

Now—after the CARD act the consumer has to EXPRESSLY opt in to permit the issuer to process over limit transactions. If you, the consumer, do tell your credit card company that it is ok to go over limit you, the consumer, can change your mind later and opt out.

There are numerous other changes brought about by the CARD act.

You can look them up at www.whitehous.gov/the_press_office/Fact-Sheet-Reforms-to-Protect-American-Credit-Card-Holders.

Be ambitious! Look it up!

16

Different types of Credit Scores

So let us talk a bit about the different credit scores for different industries that are out there.

Different industries care differently about certain items on credit reports.

Three easy ones to explain:

Bank/credit card industries: They are much more concerned with how you handle your credit card payments and have a specific FICO scoring system to reflect that.

Auto finance companies: How you have handled your car payment plays a much larger role in your credit score when applying for an auto loan. The auto finance industry has it's own FICO scoring system.

Mortgage companies: Mortgage and home loan companies have mortgage payment histories weighted more heavily and thus have a FICO scoring system to reflect that.

Don't misunderstand: It is still a FICO system and still principally works the same way as any FICO scoring system it's just that there are different score cards that calculate scores differently for different industries.

This alone can explain one of the reasons that credit scores can vary from one application to another.

A credit score can be requested when applying for an auto loan and the same day that consumer can apply for a mortgage loan (wow that person is seriously looking at pain to do that in the same day) and have two different FICO scores.

Also a consumer can apply for a mortgage loan at two different mortgage companies (again asking for pain and suffering in my opinion) and have two different credit scores.

This is usually due to different software upgrades. If the credit report company isn't running on the exact same version of FICO software then scores will be different.

This is probably BORING! But it is important.

There are other scores out there too. This one really burns my candle to the bottom!

WEBSITES, WEBSITES, everywhere. Score this, free credit that, blah blah blah!

Ok young consumer, which credit scoring website should you use.

NONE!

Please feel free to go to annualcreditreport.com and request copies of your three credit reporting agency reports.

Get a free (no strings attached) report from Transunion, Equifax, and Experian.

DO NOT pay to have a credit score issued.

WHY?

YES, I AM YELLING THIS AT YOU. SO LISTEN UP!

The credit scores that are issued at these many, many websites are not FICO scores. Most of them are Vantage or other types of scores which often are scoring systems that the credit bureaus came up with to compete with FICO.

How's that working for you guys and gals?

Well the credit reporting agencies are making gobs and I mean a ton of money from the sale of these other credit scores. The scores are not FICO scores. Did I already say that?

It bears repeating. These other scores are NOT generally used in USA lending institutions. These other scores can be very different from FICO scores. They can be much higher and usually are not lower than real FICO scores.

This is very misleading to the good old consumer who has no clue that this is not a FICO score.

I have to repeat this to almost every client that I have, most of whom have paid for a credit score online. A credit score that is misleading. So misleading in fact that there is about to be a class action lawsuit suing for the lack of disclosure about these FAKE scores. I think I'll nickname them FAKO scores. Just for fun.

Of course somewhere in the very small print it is said that this is a "whatever" type of score but it is very hard to find and thus very misleading.

I have even told some bank manager's that these aren't FICO scores and had bank manager's not believe me. The scary fact about that is again the HUGE lack of education for the consumer. Even those in the credit industry don't know some of this stuff.

Look it up. Pick any one of those websites and read the entire fine print. I dare you!

This leads to another thing. Paying for credit monitoring services. It is not necessary as a rule. However if you want to pay between $12-$30 per month at a credit monitoring service so that you can see your credit monthly then go ahead. These sites are most certainly useful to keep track of exactly what is reporting on your credit. But you may go to annualcreditreport.com once per year and pull the three reports for free. You can go every four months and pull one of the three and thus 3 times per year you could have a look at a credit report to see if there is anything funny going on.

By the way if you are reading this it would be a great idea for you to go to annualcreditreport.com and see if anything shows up on your credit now.

*Note to all readers: annualcreditscore.com is indeed free and you can get reports from Trans Union, Equifax and Experian once per year at no cost, however this is a very cumbersome website and often the reports are 30-40 pages EACH in length. *

17

Income for the credit reporting agencies

Now we come to the income portion of the story.

How do these credit reporting agencies make their money? Transunion, Experian and Equifax are not GOVERNMENT agencies. This is another fallacy that the poor old consumer doesn't realize.

Every single website that is available for consumers are there for the purpose of making the credit reporting agency, who owns it, money! Lots of money! The website charges the consumer a fee and voila, makes some serious amounts of coin.

Remember earlier we were talking about soft inquiries? Every time one is pulled the CRA (Credit Reporting Agencies for those who aren't keeping up) who issues the report gets paid. Each and every car loan, mortgage inquiry, credit card application etc all pay for the privilege of getting a credit report.

When a credit card company sends out a pre-screened offer of credit, the credit card company has paid for the list of pre-screened folks. You've likely gotten some of those yourself or you've seen them come for your parents. We get many offers for credit cards. WEEKLY!

Let's say that you own ABC Credit Cards and you want to market an offer for a new credit card to people that have a 680 or higher credit score and specifically to those folks with that score that live in Kootenai county Idaho. You literally order that "pre-screened" list from Equifax (as an example). Equifax pulls credit (a soft inquiry which will not damage a credit score) and prepares the list for ABC Credit Cards. Equifax will earn quite a lovely fee for doing so and you, owner of ABC Credit Cards, now have the list so that you can market your offer to them.

As a consumer (teenager or otherwise) you may get a the little flyer in the mail (or maybe your parents do) telling you or them about the big sale at the local car dealership and that you or they are pre-approved for the purchase of a car. Likely that auto dealer has paid one or more of the Credit Reporting Agencies for a list of clients that fits a particular demographic (segment of people who fit what the credit score market that the auto dealer is looking for). The list for the auto dealer is created by performing a soft inquiry to build a list for marketing purposes.

Because the CRA's have addresses, types of credit, credit scores, amounts of loans, dates of loans, etc. at their disposal the credit bureaus can and will sell data whenever possible. It is a huge revenue stream.

Note: the credit bureaus will not sell Social Security numbers.

18

Identity theft

Now let's have a little chat about identity theft. It is not nearly as rampant as it is made out to be. Please don't pay some company to "protect" you against identity theft. That is JUST MY OPINION.

You may not at any time bring a lawsuit against me saying that I told you not to protect yourself. Sign here.

_____ :-)

You should in fact keep quite close track of your Social Security number and of the various ways it could get swiped (slang for stolen). Again by checking your credit on a regular basis you will know if someone has used your Social without your permission.

If you do find out that someone has used your Social Security number for some purpose (and it wasn't you who used it) then file a police report. IMMEDIATLEY!

Credit cards are another story as are debit cards. Credit card and debit card numbers get stolen regularly and by many methods. I sure don't understand it but then again I'm not of the 'thief" mindset.

Recently there were devices discovered at a local gas station (close to where I live) that were for the purpose of copying and transmitting credit card and debit card numbers to the thieves. They had literally attached a device inside the gas pumps. Who thinks these things up?

It's crazy the ways that thieves can steal credit card information and debit card information.

Most of the time when credit card numbers get stolen it is caught and or flagged" by the bank whom has issued the credit. If the institution does catch it they will call or email you and tell you of "suspicious activity". When and if that happens give them a call.

But, call the number listed on the back of your card (credit, visa debit or whatever). If you call the number of the back of the card then you will not be sucked into some kind of online or telephone hoax. Typically if you call and the activity is not your activity then the bank/credit issuer will put a hold on or reverse those transactions. They will usually cancel the card as well and issue you a new one.

I have personally experienced this a number of times. Once I supposedly tried to rent a car In Ireland. The interesting thing is that I have never been to Ireland. I wish I had tried to rent a car in Ireland. It would have meant I was having lots of fun. Sorry, got off track there again.

The good news is that it never cost me a dime (or a dollar for that matter) because I was on top of things and made the appropriate phone calls once I became aware of the fraudulent activity.

But again, as a consumer you must be vigilant in logging into your bank account, your credit card accounts, any of your accounts, to keep track of all things that are showing up.

Look you know how to "login" right? Or get an app for that? Of course you do. If you don't know how to do that then please call me and I'll help with that. No wait. Please don't call unless only 10 of you buy this book then I will have time to take your calls. I'm hoping that every student in this country reads this book though and then I don't think I'll be able to take all of those calls. Just keep track. OK?

Of course if you happen to lose a credit card or debit card you should immediately call the institution (or go in person) and get it cancelled and another one issued. This protects you from anyone else trying to use your card. Again keep track of things in your life.

If you are a fortunate person who gets to go on vacation please call your bank (again use the number on the back of your card) and let them know that you are going and where you are going. Remember that I said banks have entire fraud departments looking for charges on debit/ credit cards that are unusual. That means if you suddenly start making charges in Texas when you actually live in Washington, the bank may flag it. They may put a stop on your card. This will be considered suspicious activity and you may not be able to use your card which will really inhibit the good time you will have while on vacation.

19

Beware of fees

Fees. The companies who lend you money or give you "credit" love to make fees.

To be fair it is how they make a living but many fees that consumers pay are very unnecessary and very expensive as well.

Some other things to be aware of with regard to credit card fees:

Cash advances on credit cards.

What is a cash advance? Basically when you go to the ATM or the bank and take a withdrawal of cash off of your credit card you are taking a cash advance. This is different from making a purchase on the credit card.

The minute, no the second, that you take a cash advance on a credit card you are being charged interest on that money. Usually there is also a cash advance fee of a certain amount as well (sometimes up to a 5% charge)

This differs from a purchase made on a credit card because when you make a purchase you are basically borrowing money from the credit card issuer at no charge until the due date.

If you do not pay the balance in full interest starts accruing on the balance on the card from the date that you made the purchase (A little more about that in a minute).

If you take a cash advance, there will be extra fees and interest as a result.

Fees and interest on a cash advance start from the date

of the cash advance and will accrue even if you pay the balance in full by the due date.

Yes you are borrowing the money.

Yes it belongs to the credit card issuer

Yes they will charge you interest.

Yes the rate will usually be quite high.

If you are a happy person and want to add to the profits of the credit card company by all means go ahead take a cash advance.

Just give the CEO (the head dude or dudette) a bigger bonus! Why not?

Because my friend, it is a TOTAL waste of money.

There are times in emergency when folks have no choice but to take a cash advance but it should be really a last resort. It is a very expensive proposition.

READ MY LIPS (if you could see them you could). Don't pay unnecessary fees or interest if you can avoid it! EVER!

Let's get back to borrowing the money and not paying it back in full on or before the due date.

This is where it gets a bit confusing.

OK here goes:

You charge the cool new rocking pair of jeans on the credit card.

The credit card company lends you the money to do so. Yes they are making you a loan to buy those jeans and wear them now...for free until the bill comes due.

You get the bill. The bill is due on the 12th and that is the only charge and the only balance on the card.

You pay the card in full on the 10th. Done.

No extra fee. No interest. Nothing else to deal with! Right? You basically got an interest free loan from the bank to buy and wear your new jeans! YAHOO!

You feel bad for the poor credit card issuer you say? HA! I laugh at you and with you!

The credit card issuer got paid a fee from the merchant for your swipe of the card.

Every single time you use the credit card the merchant (the store you were shopping at) pays a fee to the institution. Wow! They know how to make money eh?

That does explain why some small businesses don't accept credit cards. It actually cuts into the price of the item that is being sold.

Ok...now different scenario:

You charge same said cool pair of rocking new jeans on credit card. We are still assuming no other purchases, no previous balances, blah blah blah.

Ok...so the bill comes for same said rocking pair of jeans.

The bill is still due on the 12th. You decide you don't have the full amount available to pay the bill in full.

MAKE SURE YOU PAY AT LEAST THE MINIMUM PAYMENT OR THERE WILL BE MORE CONSEQUENCES (negatively impact your credit, get charged more fees, being irresponsible, getting a smack in the back of the head, oh wait not allowed to do that)

Let's get back to not paying the balance in full.

You pay 1/2. Guess what my friend! You are going to pay interest. Now here comes the tricky part. The interest starts from the original date of the purchase of the rocking jeans.

No free loan. No free borrowing of money from the bank. The interest goes back and starts adding up.

You decide to pay the rest of the balance once you get the next bill.

The bill has a cutoff date of say the 10th of the current month (we will use September) and still a due date of the 12th of next month. You get the bill on the September 14th because the mail didn't get it to you until then.

You decide hey...I'll pay it before the 12th of October in full. Because this chick whose book I read said to pay it in full before the due date. She must be right. So you send in the balance from the September statement on the 10th of October. Done right?

WRONG!!! NOT!!! STOP THE PRESSES!!!!

"But this chick said I would be done?" You shout.

"That was before there was a previous balance" shouts back chick who wrote the book.

The cutoff date and print date of the bill was the 10th of September and you paid the bill on October 10th.

Guess what happened between the billing date, September 10th, and the payment date, October 10th?

Interest has accrued on those days. YUP...for sure!! More interest. Now will come next month's bill with some more interest even though you have paid off the previous balance in full because you didn't pay it in full on the cutoff date.

Confusing?

You are right about that!

It is all in the lovely very tiny small print listed on the credit card issuer's application forms and disclosure forms.

Wow...this is a money maker for the old credit card issuers! YA THINK?

About the only way to avoid this *very frustrating and confusing* situation is by calling the issuer and asking for the balance as of the day you are calling and by paying the bill over the phone that same day.

It really is confusing! Always pay your bill in full. No confusion then.

The cash advance situation is the same. Except the interest has no "grace period" so to speak. It starts immediately.

Wow I have a headache now from trying to explain this without some kind of spread sheet and Power Point presentation.

Short story:

Pay bill in full before due date

Take no cash advances

Pay no interest

Credit card companies will periodically send you pretty little "convenience checks" as well. Those checks can and will be considered cash advances. Many times they will come with a one-time transaction fee as well. Beware that those little checks issued for your "convenience" will again be very costly.

While we are still in the credit card mode let's talk about foreign transaction fees. Ok...this will pertain to your credit cards and also your bank card that can be used like a credit card. Again you are a lucky person and your parents are paying for you to travel to Brazil. Why Brazil you ask? I really don't know except that it sounds quite exotic and I've heard that it is very beautiful. If you don't want to go to Brazil then pick someplace out in your mind (use that imagination) and pick another foreign country. And no, Arkansas is not a foreign country. To those readers in Arkansas please take no offense (no lawsuits allowed: __sign here_____). None is intended!!

Anyway you are traveling to Brazil or where ever. Your parents are paying the entire trip (we all want those type of parents don't we?) except for your spending money. You don't have a lot of cash but you are going to Brazil and you are taking your shiny new credit card or bank Visa/Master card debit card with you. You get to Brazil and the first thing you do is hit up the local bank machine because you need some cash. You take a cash advance off of your credit card. *** Note to self, see the above cautions regarding cash advances***

Or you use your debit card and withdraw money from your account. The money comes out in Brazilian Real. That is the name of the money in Brazil. I'm not kidding! It really is the name of the money in Brazil!

Anyway...the bank/credit card company or whatever is going to charge you some fees.

1-The bank where you withdrew the money will charge a fee for using their machine.

The amount of the fee will depend on the financial institution

2-The bank/credit card issuer that your card comes from will charge an exchange rate.

Exchange rates are fairly similar from institution to institution and are something that you can neither negotiate, nor get away from.

3-Your institution will likely charge you another fee for using a machine that isn't theirs.

This can be a few dollars and will vary according to who you bank with.

4-A foreign transaction fee can be charged. This is very common and can range from 3 to 7 percent of the amount of the purchase or withdrawal.

Not all credit card companies charge foreign transaction fees. If you are traveling abroad then it would be very wise to find a bank/credit card company and a card that does not charge a foreign transaction fee.

These fees for simply using money while out of the country can add up quickly and can be a very real expense of traveling outside of the US. Be aware of the rules from your bank or credit card company before you go so that you don't have any surprises when you get your statement at home.

Debit card fees: If you go to a bank machine that isn't in your "network" meaning that your bank doesn't have an arrangement for you to withdraw from that bank machine at no cost, then you will also incur a fee for using another banks machine. Or if you use a bank machine that is in a store (and isn't part of your bank) you will pay fees. These fees are a total waste of money.

Plan ahead! Get an app or something like that. Try not to use an institution, other than the one that you bank with, if possible.

Overdraft fees. This is one that is particularly irksome to me. In some instances you can actually spend more money than you have available in your checking account. If your account balance goes negative then it's called an overdrawn account.

The bank will charge you a substantial fee for that. It could be $25 or $35 in fees called overdraft or non-sufficient funds fees. Total waste of money here folks!

It comes down to paying attention to your bank balance and your spending habits. Quite important!

20

Other types of financing

Getting away from credit cards now. Let's go on a merry path exploring other types of financing. Hold onto your hats! Here we go.

Title loans

Yikes. These are NASTY, HORRIBLE products.

Note: No title loan company is allowed to sue me. It's my opinion for heaven's sake!

Let's get back to the topic! Shall we?

What is a title loan? Usually it is a loan where you, the consumer, signs over the title of your vehicle, motorcycle, travel trailer or whatever to a company who gives you a lovely little "short term" loan.

RUN, HIDE, DON'T DO IT!

If there is anyone in the title loan industry reading this: I'm sorry but it just isn't the smartest way for a young person to borrow money. I'm not slamming you title loan folks. But it is factually true that borrowing money from a title loan company is VERY expensive.

Title loans come with interest rates of 100% and up. I have seen them in the 300% range.

Yes, 300%.

I'm not sure I can even calculate numbers on that without a computer program.

In a nutshell if you borrow money you will pay a LOT of interest and hardly any principal back on the loan.

Note: Principal is the amount you originally borrowed.

I am really trying to make a point here so I'm actually going onto my computer to pick some numbers and give you some kind of idea how this works. I hope.

Let's take a fairly typical title loan.

You have a car. It's value is let's say $3,500.

The title loan company will lend you approximately $1,000 if the car is paid off.

They won't usually lend more than 30-35% of the value of the vehicle so that if they have to repossess it they will be able to sell it for a profit.

An interest rate on a loan such as this might run 25% for 30 days. If you do not pay the entire loan back at the end of the 30 days it will roll over for another 30 days at another 25%. This works out to approximately 300% per year.

It isn't explained very carefully to folks that the 25% is really a monthly thing. When we put together the numbers they pencil out like this:

$1,000	original loan amount
25%	interest rate per month (most interest is calculated annually not monthly)
12	months that you need the money
$3,000	amount of interest that will be owed in 12 months

That means that for your $1,000 that you have borrowed you will have to pay back $4,000 if you keep that loan for a year. Wow...I'm in the wrong business! Maybe I should start offering up title loans. NOT likely!

Note: The calculations above are for illustration purposes only because there will be payments due on this type of loan on a monthly basis but because the rates are so high very little principal will get paid.

Hopefully this illustration will give you a very concrete reason for not getting a title loan. It is a very bad idea.

Pay Day loans.

The ads for these are all over the place.

"Need money quick? Get $200 quick until payday. Get it fast"

These ads are in the mail, on the TV, on billboards, on the internet, luring you sucking you in, making you want to be their friend. Okay maybe the last part not so much but you get the idea.

These loans can go by various names: Payday loans, post-dated check loans, check advance loans, deferred deposit loans, or cash advance loans (there is that cash advance phrase again).

No matter what moniker this type of lending uses, it remains that they are very costly and somewhat similar to Title loans.

They work like this: An unsuspecting soul walks into a payday loan place and writes a check payable to ABC Payday Loan Schmucks. ABC Payday Loan Schmucks charges a fee for said loan which is included in the amount of the check that the unsuspecting soul writes out.

Let's say unsuspecting soul wants $100 and ABC Payday Loan Schmucks have a fee of $50 for every $100 borrowed. Okay...stop right there. Doesn't that seem a bit much? $50 fee for $100 loan! WHOLLY SMOKES people! RED FLAG, PURPLE FLAG, BLACK FLAG!!

Anyway on with the story! ABC Payday Loan Schmucks indeed might be charging such a fee. Unsuspecting soul who really needs $100 for something writes the check for the total amount, in this case $150. ABC Payday Loan Schmucks agree to hold the check until the loan is due which is usually the next payday for unsuspecting soul. Thus the very original: "Payday loan" term. ABC Payday Loan Schmucks deposit the loan amount into unsuspecting soul's account less the fee. In this case $100 crisp dollars goes into unsuspecting soul's account. ABC Payday Loan Schmucks make the agreement with unsuspecting soul to debit their account on that payday. The amount debited on the payday is the full amount owed. In this particular case it would be $150. If unsuspecting soul extends the loan or doesn't have the funds to pay the whole amount back then the loan is extended. Usually it is extended for the same fee which was used to borrow the funds in the first place.

Let's for sake of argument give ABC Payday Loan Schmucks a bit of a break and say that they are only charging $15 for the same $100 lent to unsuspecting soul. Unsuspecting soul says on payday "wait I don't have enough, Can I pay this back on my next payday in two weeks?"

"Of course!" Said the very nice lady at ABC Payday Loan Schmucks.

The loan rolls over and another $15 is charges for the next 14 days. If unsuspecting soul continues on this path and extends the loan a total of 3 times the finance charge would be a total of $60. $15 charge for the initial loan, and $15 x 3 for each of the 3 extensions.

Unsuspecting soul has now paid $60 to borrow $100. That works out to an annual percentage rate of 391 percent.

RED FLAG, GREEN FLAG, PURPLE FLAG. STOP!!!

The alternatives to Payday loans and Title loans can be much cheaper. A small loan from your Credit union, a small loan company or your bank would be a much cheaper solution. If you need to get a loan from a bank, credit union or small loan company and you want it to be affordable then you will need, guess what? Wait for it! GOOD CREDIT! DECENT FICO SCORES! See how I did that? Brought it all back around to the beginning here.

21

Scams

There are numerous collection agencies out there that will try to "pull one over" on consumers.

Frequently I work with clients that have had collection agencies call them to ask for payments on an old collection account.

There are a number of things that are important when you are contacted by a collection agency.

Make sure that the debt really exists. Quite often I will get a call from a client that is confused. "I just got a call from ABC Collections. I've never heard of these guys. They are telling me that I owe $2,000 and I don't remember owing that much to anyone."

Frequently we have short memories so not all of these calls are a scam. Many of them are however.

If you get such a call there are a couple of things to do first.

Get the name and address and telephone number of the company and person calling.

Google that company and find out what is says on the internet about them.

Call the number back to see who answers. This is a good one. Often when we call back the number it isn't for a company at all.

If all of the above items check out then ask for a full accounting of this bill that you owe. If it is a legitimate collection then by law they have to provide a full accounting of the ORIGINAL debt if you request it. If the collection agency doesn't want to give you a full accounting of the original debt then that is a red flag.

If the company is using very threatening language and telling you that they are coming to take away your personal items (car etc.) that is another red flag. It is against the law to use threatening language and tactics.

The company calling threatens to put you in jail. They are not allowed to do that. Immediately ask for phone numbers, debt verifications and who you are speaking to. Then hang up.

Scenario: If the debt is previously paid.

When paying off a collection with a collection agency always ask for a letter to show that it has been paid. This will be your future proof if necessary. That along with your bank records are the records that you need to keep to protect yourself. Make sure that you pay the debt with some form of payment that you can track in the future if necessary.

This one happens a lot as well. A client will get a call on a bill that is already paid. Tell the person that you are speaking to that it has been paid to a different collection agency.

Do step 4 in the example above. Ask for proof. If anything is legitimate then they should have no trouble providing you with proof of the debt. If the collection agency does provide proof then send them the letter that shows you paid it with another company.

Sometimes when you pay a collection off the collection agency fails to notify the original creditor (the person who lent you the money or that you owe the money to originally) that it has been paid. It would be wise of you to make sure that you keep good records and check your credit about 45 days after you pay the collection off to make sure that it is showing as paid as well as showing to the original creditor that it is now a zero balance.

If the debt was included in a bankruptcy:

This also happens quite a lot. A debt is included in bankruptcy and for any number of reasons it doesn't show up that way on a credit report.

If this happens you will want to send a copy of your bankruptcy paperwork to the original creditor to make sure that they change the reporting to the credit bureaus.

It can happen for a number of reasons that it is reporting incorrectly. It could be that the attorney has not done the appropriate paperwork. It could be that the creditor has not notified the credit reporting agencies.

This can also be a scam of sorts. I just had a client call (five minutes ago...really!!!) that was getting a collection notice from a collection company. The name of the collection company is legitimate. However the debt that they are trying to collect for is not. It was included in the client's bankruptcy over 5 years ago. It is not legal to try to collect on a debt that was included in a bankruptcy.

YIKEs! Consumers are expected to know ALL OF THIS STUFF? REALLLY? They sure are!

By the way, YOU are the consumer!

This doesn't even touch on the world of email scams which could be another entire book. Yikes.

22

Ignoring bills in the mail

Balance due notices of bills in the mail: They aren't a big deal. SERIOUSLY??????

You had to go to Emergency because you cut your big toe down at the beach while jumping off of logs and it was very ouchy. 3 months ago.

There goes my grammar again. My English teacher would be very upset at me!

You gave the hospital your medical card and that was that. They put a pink bandage, with little purple teddy bears on it, on your big toe and you were happy as a lark (I have no idea how happy larks are) and went along your merry way.

Let's fast forward 3 months: You get a bill in the mail for $1,225. It's from the hospital. You think: I'm not paying that. "My medical insurance should pay for it!" You shove "THE BILL" into a drawer and forget about it. You IGNORE the bill!

Fast forward 2 additional months: You get a notice from a collection agency that this bill is now turned over to them and that the collection agency is collecting on behalf of the hospital.

Again your brain says "My medical insurance was supposed to pay for it". You again IGNORE "the bill".

Fast forward 3 more months. You have received many calls from this collection agency. You put a block on your phone so that those calls cannot come through. You have shredded any more notices that come from the collection agency.

This time a notice from an attorney comes and they are filing a judgment against you. A court case date has been set. You IGNORE that too.

A judgment gets filed and then a couple more months go by.

A garnishment for your wages is issued...

Is this scenario starting to sound scary yet? Well it is sounding scary to me. And it IS scary. And it HAS HAPPENED to clients of mine. I had one gal completely ignore all of the collection notices, the court date, and the judgment. She called me in a panic by the time it got to the point of the garnishment.

** If you don't know what that means simply put: your wages are taken by the court and applied against the outstanding debt. And you have no choice as to the amount of the garnishment**

By the time this gal called me it was WAY TOO LATE TO DO ANYTHING ABOUT IT.

Moral of this story: DO NOT IGNORE NOTICES THAT YOU OWE MONEY.

If you get a notice that you owe money then please don't assume it will go away if you ignore it. It won't go away or get dealt with by ignoring it. The results of ignoring it could be very detrimental.

Just recently a medical bill came to my home for a procedure that was performed on my husband. It should have been covered by medical. When I called the company who sent us the bill I found out that the reason it wasn't covered is because the insurance company had him listed as a female. Claim denied.

If we hadn't called the company who sent the bill and then followed up with our medical insurance to get this corrected then this would have gone to a collection agency and possibly impacted our credit in a negative way.

You have to be the one to do the work here folks. The gang at the local collection agency doesn't really care what your excuses are. Really they don't. They have heard them all and are immune to them too.

I really want for you to understand that you cannot ignore something just because it's unpleasant. I'm not your parent, nor am I trying to raise you. But, when it comes to your credit and keeping it in good, or great, shape you are in charge of making sure that things get handled correctly. If you are not sure how to handle something then email me (yes you really can) and I will either put you in touch with a reputable credit repair company or have someone from my company point you in the right direction.

23

Conclusion

In Conclusion:

Wow, I sound like a lawyer a bit. I sometimes I wish I were a lawyer so that I could fight for people and kick the bad guys who want to take advantage of the credit consumer in the butt! But I digress. Sorry!

If I have put you to sleep I sincerely apologize for doing so. It's not supposed to work that way. Hopefully you were awake through the majority of the ramblings.

If you get nothing at all out of this book, then that would totally suck! If you do, and I sure hope that you do then, the following items would be the ones that I would rank as the most important:

1- Pay your bills on time or before the due date. If you pay them before they are due it does not give you extra credit points but it does ensure that the payment is not late. However, if it is paid late then it could have a negative impact on your credit score and or cause you to pay a late fee.

2- Don't ignore something that comes in the mail just because you believe it's incorrect. Follow up and follow through.

3- Take care of your credit. It's your baby. It can make your life miserable or it can help make it better. You need it to function in today's world.

4- Even though I list co-signing as a way to help you build credit please don't co-sign anything for anyone yourself unless you are in charge of making the payments. This is the only way you can actually ensure that the payments are made on time and that they are not impacting your credit in a negative way. Just don't co-sign

Everyone who might be confused about the statement above please RAISE your hand!! I can't see you but you will feel better if you raise your hand. I'm sure of it.

5- Don't pay any bank interest or fees for anything that you do not have to. If you pay off the credit card in full before or on the due date you won't pay any interest to the bank.

6- Credit is like a pizza. Take care of the parts you like the most first (pepperoni—payment history, cheese—amount of revolving debt you carry) and the rest will eventually get eaten (be ok)

24

Definitions/Glossary

Algorithm
-A set of functions or mathematical rules performed in a specific order to compute a result. (computer programming rules)

Cash Advance
-The process that allows the credit card holder (the consumer) to withdraw cash from the available limit on the credit card. Withdrawn either from an ATM, by check or at a branch of the credit card issuer (if applicable)

Collection(s)
-An obligation that goes unpaid and is delinquent as a result. It is eventually sent to "collection" or becomes a "collection account"

Credit
-Money that a bank or business will allow an individual to borrow with the promise of paying it back in the future

-A record of how well you have paid your bills in the past

(In this book we will be using the term CREDIT with both definitions)

Credit Reporting Agencies
-A business that maintains a record of an individual's and/or a business's credit history

Credit Score
-A number assigned to a person's credit history that indicates to lenders their likelihood of becoming 90 days or more delinquent on a debt

Delinquent (delinquency)
-In this book: when a payment is made after the due date it becomes "delinquent". It is past due based on the agreed upon payment date.

FICO
-Credit scoring software that is used by the majority of lenders in the USA for decisions in lending money.

It is also sometimes used to screen job applicants, insurance applicants, rental applications among other things.

Finance
-To borrow money from a source with the promise to pay it back to the lender sometime in the future

Finances
-The personal management of money and credit
-A balance of assets and liabilities

Garnishment
-When a court order is issued to withhold wages from payroll in order to pay an outstanding debt. This can happen for many types of debts.

Child support, Judgments, and taxes are a few examples.

Interest

-Charges for borrowing money expressed in a percentage that is payable in addition to the principal that was borrowed.

Judgment

-A legal ruling or finding.

In the case of credit it will pertain to an unpaid obligation that a judge will rule is owed to whoever the plaintiff is.

Lender

-An institution or a person who lends money to an individual or an entity with the intent that it be paid back (in the case of this book, with interest)

Mortgage

-A **mortgage loan**, also referred to as a **mortgage**, is used by purchasers of a home to raise funds to buy real estate.

Payment history

-A record detailing the dates that payments are made on an outstanding financial obligation.

Pre-screened

-The process of obtaining a list of a particular segment of the population for the purpose of marketing to that particular populace a specific product or service

Principal

-The original amount borrowed or owed prior to any interest or fees being added.

T.A. Jensen is a certified credit expert and is the owner of CPR Credit Repair.

She has been in the mortgage, credit and banking industries since 1988.

Ms. Jensen is happily married and has one daughter. She loves to run, cycle and do the occasional triathlon.